West Germany is my country

In this book 26 people from all over West Germany tell you what their life is like—life in the cities, life in industry, and life in the country.

WEST GERMANY
is my country

Bernice and Cliff Moon

My Country

America is my country
Argentina is my country
Australia is my country
Britain is my country
China is my country
Denmark is my country
France is my country
Greece is my country
India is my country

Israel is my country
Italy is my country
Japan is my country
Kenya is my country
New Zealand is my country
Spain is my country
The European U.S.S.R.
West Germany is my country

Further titles are in preparation

This book is based on We live in West Germany,
in Wayland's 'Living Here' series, by Christa Stadtler.
The cover photograph was supplied by PICTUREPOINT—LONDON.
The photograph on page 41 was supplied
by Bruce Coleman Ltd/David Davies, and the
one on page 51 by Ullstein Bilderdienst.

First published in 1985 by
Wayland (Publishers) Ltd
49 Lansdowne Place, Hove
East Sussex BN3 1HF, England

© Copyright 1985 Wayland (Publishers) Ltd

ISBN 0 85078 613 4

Phototypeset by Latimer Trend & Company Ltd, Plymouth
Printed in Italy by G. Canale & C.S.p.A., Turin
Bound in the UK by The Bath Press

Contents

I am Dieter.
I'm a pilot.

I work for a German airline called Lufthansa and
I fly planes from Frankfurt airport.
Frankfurt is in the heart of West Germany.
About 300 Lufthansa planes take off and land here every day.

I fly Boeing 737s like this one.

The two main West German motorways meet at Frankfurt.

I was a co-pilot for ten years and then, two years ago,
I became a captain and now I fly about 600 hours a year.
I enjoy my work even though I have to be away
from my home and family for 2 to 5 days at a time.
Before each flight I talk to my crew and my co-pilot
about the trip and the route we will be taking.
I have to order the fuel and check the weather forecasts.
In bad weather our equipment allows us to land
when we can see only 50 metres (55 yards) ahead.

I am Walter and I'm a woodcarver.

I live in a village called Oberammergau in the Bavarian Alps.
Oberammergau is famous because every ten years
the villagers put on a special play about the death of Christ.
The play lasts for almost eight hours and people come
from all over the world to see it.

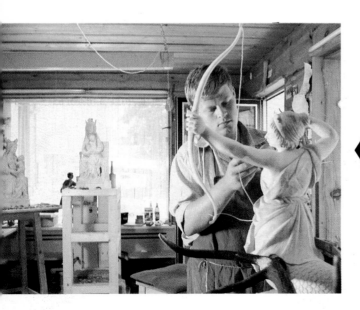

Our village is also well known
for its wood carvings.
Here you can see me
finishing a carving
in my workshop.

Most of the houses in this part of Germany have
a wooden statue of the Virgin Mary and the baby Jesus
beside a candle and a vase of flowers in one of the rooms.
Sometimes a small wooden figure of Christ on the cross
hangs above the dining table as well.
Bavarian farmers used to do a lot of wood carving in winter
when their fields were covered with snow.
Nowadays there are about 500 woodcarvers in the Alps and
over 100 of them work here in Oberammergau.

Many houses in Bavaria have pictures painted on the walls.

I'm Astrid and I'm a baker.

Every morning I start
baking at 4 a.m.
I bake fifteen kinds
of bread and rolls.
The bread has to be ready
by 7 o'clock.

The flour we use is made
from wheat which is grown
on farms like this one
in southern Germany.

When we make bread rolls we put small pieces of dough
onto baking trays and then we put the trays into the oven.

West Germans who want to be bakers, butchers and cooks
work with a firm as an apprentice for three years.
During that time they go to college for one day a week.
At the end of three years they take an exam and
if they pass they are qualified to do their job.
I've just passed my exam and now I plan to leave home
to open a bakery in a Third World country.

I am Jürgen.
I'm a soldier.

Every West German male must serve in the army for 15 months.
Anyone who doesn't agree to this has to work for 18 months
in a hospital or a home for the sick or elderly.
I joined the army after I'd finished my apprenticeship.
I'm 23 years old now and I'll go to university
after I've left the army.
We need an army because we are afraid that one day
the Russians will attack along the East German or
Czechoslovakian borders with our country.
If that ever happens we will be helped by NATO forces
which are based in West Germany.

We are always having
to tighten the tracks
on our tanks because
they become loose from
driving over rough ground.

I share a room with
four other soldiers.
We play cards a lot
when we're off duty.

I'm Joseph and I'm a miner.

I work at the Fortuna coal mine near Cologne.
There is more lignite (brown coal) in this area
than in any other part of Europe.
We mine about 120 million tonnes of lignite each year and
most of it is used by the local power stations,
which produce a quarter of West Germany's electricity.

Fortuna is an opencast
mine and the coal is dug
out of the ground by
excavators like this.

Opencast mining leaves huge holes in the ground.
When all the coal has been mined, the hole is filled in
and planted with forests.

Sometimes there are farms, woods and villages on the land
where we want to start mining.
They all disappear when the excavators move in and
since 1945, 26,000 people and 72 villages have had to move.

My name is Jutta. I'm a schoolgirl.

I am 11 years old and I am in my final year
at primary school in Munich, the capital of Bavaria.
Today I am using an overhead projector in my classroom.

We have a party at the end of the summer term and
our parents come to school to help prepare the food.

There are only two comprehensive schools in Bavaria so
we either go to a *gymnasium* or to a 'main school'
when we leave primary school.
Gymnasiums are for children who will later go to university and
main schools are for those who will leave at 16
to start an apprenticeship.

School starts at 8 a.m. and ends at 1 p.m.
We get about two hours homework each day and
there are gym and needlework lessons in the afternoons.
We have six weeks' holiday in the summer and
most of us go to the mountains and lakes
because Munich gets very hot in summer.

I am Heinz and I'm a wine-maker.

I grow vines and make wine at Valwig in the Mosel Valley.
German vines are grown along the banks of the River Rhine and
smaller rivers like the Neckar, Main, Mosel and Ahr.
This part of West Germany is ideal for growing vines.
We get enough rain in the growing season from May to August
and warm weather in autumn when the grapes are ripening.

 I have to check that
the vines aren't diseased
or covered in insects.
We spray them in summer
to keep them healthy.

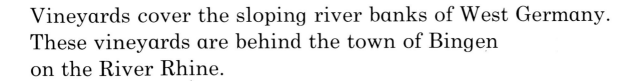

Vineyards cover the sloping river banks of West Germany.
These vineyards are behind the town of Bingen
on the River Rhine.

My family has owned vineyards for 300 years.
We also have cellars for storing our wine and
a bottling factory which produces 3 million bottles a year.
Over half of our wine is sold in Germany and
the rest is exported all over the world.

My name is Robert. I'm a mayor.

I have been the Mayor
of Lübeck since 1976.
Lübeck is the busiest port
on the Baltic coast
of West Germany.
The city is governed by a
Senate and a Parliament.
The Senate runs the city and
the Parliament decides how
the money from taxes
should be spent.

The *Holstentor* gate was
built in 1447.
It is at the entrance
to the old town.

Lübeck has more old houses than all the other north German
cities put together and one of my most important jobs
is to look after the preservation of these lovely buildings.
We spend a great deal of money on new shops and roads
as well as on modernizing the insides of old houses.
We only knock down the old houses when they are unsafe or
when there is no other route for new roads.

Nowadays Lübeck is a mixture of old and new.
We have modern shops, offices and car parks alongside
well-preserved old houses and churches.

I am Robert and I'm a skipper.

I am the skipper of a barge called the *Genoveva*.
We sail up and down the River Rhine from
Rotterdam in Holland to Basel in Switzerland.
The Rhine is one of the longest and busiest rivers in Europe.
It is 1,320 km (820 miles) long and it takes us
about eight days to sail upstream from Rotterdam to Basel.
Sailing downstream only takes us about three days
because we have the current to help us.

I live on the barge with
my wife and children.
It is the only home
we have and we never
take a holiday.

Barges on the Rhine carry oil, coal and building materials.
It is much cheaper to transport things by water
than by road or rail.
We sail all day from about five o'clock in the morning
until ten or eleven o'clock in the evening.

We sail through the beautiful city of Cologne
on our way up and down the Rhine.

I am Herbert.
I'm a manager.

I'm a manager at the BMW car factory in Munich.
There are two other BMW factories in Bavaria.

These cars are almost ready for the showrooms.
We have to check that everything is working properly.

Munich is a large, busy city but you don't have to go far
to find lovely Bavarian scenery like this.

About 47,000 people work in BMW factories and in 1983
we built over 400,000 cars.
We can't build cars fast enough and you would have to wait
about eight months if you ordered a BMW now.
There is also a large electrical goods factory in Munich
as well as small factories which print books,
make clothes and brew beer.
There is less unemployment in Munich than in other parts
of West Germany.

My name is Karin. I'm an M.P.

I am 30 years old and I've been an M.P. since 1983.
We formed a new party called the Greens in 1980 and
we won 26 seats in the March 1983 elections.
We believe in banning nuclear weapons and making sure
that factories don't pollute the air or kill plants and animals.
We are trying to make West Germany a better place to live in.

I work in an office
which overlooks the Rhine
and the city of Bonn,
the capital of West Germany.

There are four other parties in the West German Parliament:
the Christian Democratic Union, the Christian Socialist Union,
the Free Democratic Party and the Social Democratic Party.
We have two parliamentary chambers:
the *Bundestag* and the *Bundesrat*.
There are 519 members of the *Bundestag*.
The *Bundesrat* has only 45 members and their job is to
advise the *Bundestag* about new laws.
I spend much of my time working on the committee
which deals with women's rights and youth problems.

My home is in Duisburg on the River Rhine.
Duisburg has the largest inland port in Europe.

My name is Karl.
I'm a truck driver.

I spend up to five days a week in my truck.
There is a bunk-bed in the cab so I only go home at weekends.
Most of the time I carry goods between Stuttgart and Berlin.
West Berlin belongs to West Germany, but
it is surrounded by East Germany.
There are very strict rules for anyone who drives there.
I am not allowed to leave the motorway without permission and
the police check my truck carefully on every trip.
I drive about 150,000 km (93,000 miles) a year but
that's not too difficult because we have so many motorways.
The first motorway in Europe was built
between Cologne and Bonn in 1935 and
today we have 7,300 km (4,500 miles) of motorway.

Our motorways are quiet
on Sundays because trucks
aren't allowed to use them
from midnight on Saturday
until midnight on Sunday.

After 4 hours' driving
I have to rest for 1 hour.
Then I can drive for
another 4 hours before
I must take a 12-hour rest.

I'm Martin and I'm a farmer.

My dairy farm is in southern Bavaria.
We keep 27 cows and they have to be fed and milked
at 6 a.m. and 5 p.m. every day of the year.

➡

We have a bull for breeding, but we sell
the bull calves for meat.
We keep all the heifers for their milk.
All the food for our cattle is grown here on the farm.
We make hay three times a year and grow corn and maize.
We have to take all our milk to the local dairy every day.
Most of the farmers in this part of Bavaria keep cattle
because the land is too stony and hilly for crops.

Bavarian farmhouses are very beautiful buildings.
This is where I live with my wife and children.

I am Andreas and I'm a student.

I am studying agriculture at Giessen University in the centre of West Germany. There was a university here in 1607 but the buildings we use date from 1880. There are about 16,000 students at Giessen now. Altogether there are 83 universities in West Germany with a total of about 1,121,000 students.

I use a bike to get to and from my lectures.

Beer is very popular in West Germany and I enjoy
having a drink and a chat with my friends.

Students have not had government grants since 1983 but
we can borrow money which has to be repaid
when we've finished our courses.
Many of us work during the holidays and last year
I worked on a large chicken farm.
I didn't like it because there were 15,000 chickens
kept in small cages in one large shed.
The farmer was only interested in how many eggs he could sell.
Since then I've eaten only free-range eggs and
I've been reading about how I can farm in more 'natural' ways.

I'm called Hanna and I'm a businesswoman.

I have a hut on the beach at Sierksdorf on the Baltic Coast.
From there I rent out beach chairs to holiday-makers.
The Baltic Sea is not as rough as the North Sea so
quite a few people come to this part of Germany
for their holidays between early June and the end of August.
I start getting the chairs ready at 7 a.m. and by 1 p.m.
they are usually all taken, especially on a sunny day.

My chairs are wicker and
they are shaped to protect
people from the wind.
They cost 8 DM (about £2)
a day to rent.

There are other seaside resorts on the Baltic Coast but most of them are bigger and busier than Sierksdorf.
We get a lot of families with young children as well as elderly people during our short season.
Many Germans prefer to go to Greece, Spain and Italy these days because they can have a cheap holiday and enjoy warmer, sunnier weather.

This is the beach at Sierksdorf where I rent out my chairs.

I am Gerhard.
I am a vicar.

I am the Protestant Vicar of Heidelberg University.
I came here because I wanted to work with students.

People gather at my student centre every night of the week.

Heidelberg Castle stands above the town,
overlooking the River Neckar.

We have eight meeting-rooms in the student centre and
they are fully booked every night during term time.
There are political groups as well as a group
which helps Turkish children to speak and read German.
We also have Bible-study classes and, of course, lots of parties.
I take wedding, baptism and funeral services.
If students have problems they often come to me for advice.
I do my best to help and I'm happy to say that
sometimes my friendship and advice are useful to them.

My name is Heinz. I'm a dock worker.

I work for a shipping firm in Hamburg harbour.
Hamburg is on the River Elbe,
122 km (76 miles) from the North Sea.
It is the second largest city in West Germany.
Hamburg is the home-port for half the ships
in the West German merchant fleet.

We load and unload ships
from all over the world.
We cannot deal with
modern oil tankers but
a new port is being built
at the mouth of the Elbe.

Steel for shipbuilding comes by rail from the Ruhr Valley.
The shipbuilding yards are very modern because
they were completely rebuilt after World War II.
My firm can berth twenty ships at a time and
we handle things like baskets from China, fertilizers,
rolls of paper, copper wire and sacks of rice.
We have enough work at the moment but
it won't be long before we start getting problems
because of the slump in world trade.

Hamburg is an important port and shipbuilding centre.
It also has dry docks for repairing ships.

I'm Joseph and I'm a carpenter.

My home is near Split in Yugoslavia and I visit my wife and children three or four times a year. It takes me 20 hours to drive home.
I came to Duisburg for work fifteen years ago. There are about four and a half million foreign workers in West Germany at the present time.

I am a skilled carpenter and I work for a construction firm.

There are many steelworks in Duisburg.

Duisburg is in the Ruhr Valley which has more industry
than any other part of Europe.
There is a great deal of unemployment here but I've been lucky
because my firm has had plenty of orders.
We did go on a four-day week for a time but now
we're working five days, but with no overtime.
I send as much money as I can to my family in Yugoslavia.

I'm Hanelore.
I'm a waitress.

I live in Munich and
work in a beer hall
which seats 5,000 people.
In summer we serve about
30,000 people every day.
There are 150 waiters and
waitresses and we serve
the beer in a large glass
called a *Mass* which holds
one litre (1·75 pints).
They are very heavy and
I can only carry three
or four at a time, but
some waiters can manage ten.

◀ This is where I work.

We have rooms inside and a beer garden outside
where people can drink and eat snacks.

Most of the snacks we sell are German sausages with
sauerkraut, which is shredded cabbage.
If you go to a Bavarian restaurant you will find that
one of the favourite meals is dumplings made from
bread or potatoes, which are eaten with beef or pork.
Early in October each year we have a festival in Munich
called the *Oktoberfest* and it lasts for two weeks.
About 6 million visitors come from every part of Germany
and from all over the world to eat and drink at the festival.

My name is Dieter.
I am a forester.

I work in the Black Forest, south of Baden-Baden.
We cut down trees, clear the land and plant new trees.

These trees will be sold to a local papermill.

Papermills use young trees so we cut them down
when they are 50 years old.
Builders need older, taller trees for beams and rafters.
Most of the trees are cut down in the autumn.
In winter I look after the wild animals which live in the forest.
In spring we plant new trees and repair roads and footpaths.
We also spray young trees to kill diseases and we put fences
round them so that the deer will not damage the bark.

People come to the forest for peace and exercise.
We have miles of nature walks and jogging paths
as well as lots of car parks and picnic places.

Part of my home is a hotel which is run by my wife.
People come here to have a forest holiday.

I am Konrad and I'm a traffic policeman.

I work in Lohr which isn't far from Frankfurt. I joined the police force five years ago and most of the time I deal with parking and speeding offences and accidents. Most accidents are caused by speeding and drinking, or because the driver is young and inexperienced.

The driver of this car hasn't paid the meter so I'm booking him.

I use a fast car when I go out on patrol.

In West Germany about 13,000 people are killed in
road accidents every year so the police are very strict.
There is no speed limit on our busy motorways and
that means we get some very bad pile-ups.

We also try to catch people who dump rubbish in the forests
and we have to make sure that bars close at 1 a.m.
We deal with crowd control so when there's a beer festival
we stay outside the tents in case a fight breaks out.

My name is Andrea.
I'm a teacher.

I work in a kindergarten, or nursery school, near Frankfurt.
I'm 23 years old and I used to work in a children's hospital.
We teach 100 children between the ages of 3 and 5.

We have four large rooms like this at our school.

The children come in between 8 a.m. and 9 a.m.
Many are collected at midday but parents
who work in Frankfurt often collect them at tea-time.
When the children are 6, they go to primary school.
Most of our children live in the blocks of flats behind the school.
Many of them have non-German parents.
In the centre of Frankfurt almost three-quarters of the children
belong to families who have come here from other countries.

Our kindergarten has a lovely play area in the garden.

I'm Jonathan and I'm an actor.

I work in the inns,
nightclubs and theatres
of West Berlin.
Berlin is well known
for cabaret and I'm a
cabaret artist.
I perform songs and poems
which make fun of some of
the serious and dangerous
things which are happening
in our country.

Most of the time I act
on stage on my own.

This is a checkpoint on the wall which splits Berlin
into East and West.

West Berlin is part of West Germany but it is in the centre
of East Germany, about 160 km (100 miles) from the border.
At the end of World War II, Berlin was split between Russia,
America, France and Britain but in 1948 the Americans,
French and British joined their sectors together.
The Russians then cut off all the supply routes for 14 months.
When that was over, millions of refugees tried to get from
East Germany to West Germany and so the Russians built
a concrete wall to try to stop them.

My name is Joseph. I'm a pensioner.

I'm 75 years old and I've lived in the village of Hirschau,
near Stuttgart, all my life.
I have been a football fan ever since the game started
in West Germany after World War II.
The first football match at Hirschau Sports Club was in 1951.
Nowadays every village has its own football team and
the saddest thing for me is that I was too old to be a footballer.

About 800 people lived in Hirschau before 1939 but
when the war ended lots of refugees came to live here.
That changed our lives because our new neighbours
spoke differently and had different customs and opinions.
Now there are 3,000 people in the village and many of them
have come from other parts of Germany
as well as from Italy and Yugoslavia.

Hirschau is now a mixture
of old and new houses
and buildings.

I went to the 1976
Olympics in Munich.
This is one of the stadiums
built for the Games.

I'm Sister Angelinis. I'm a nurse.

I came to the St Francis Convent in Münster in 1961. There are 190 nuns in the convent and about half of us are nurses in the St Francis Hospital.

My main job is looking after premature babies. We can't let them go home until they weigh 3 kg (6·6 lb).

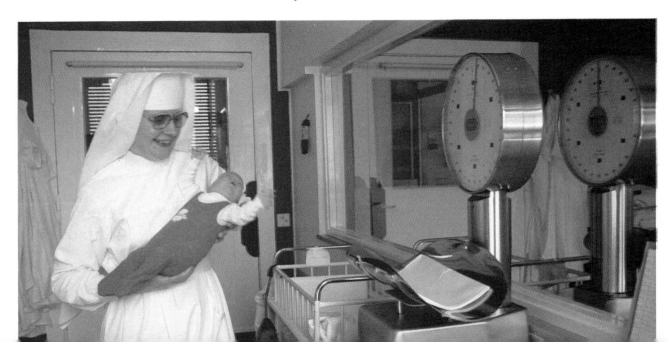

The hospital has 600 beds and a staff of over 1,000.
We also have two teachers and a schoolroom
so that children who are well enough can have lessons.

I start work at 7 a.m. and work until early evening
with a midday break for lunch and prayers.

We try to cure the children's illnesses but we also try to make
them feel happy and comfortable while they are here with us.

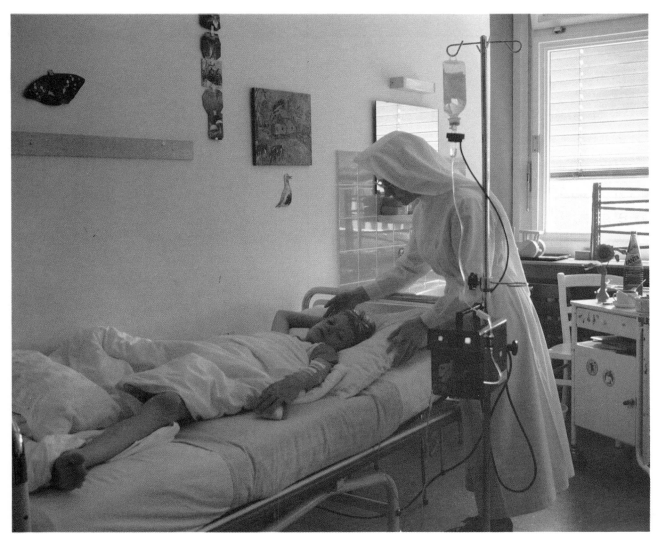

My name is Peter and I am a radio producer.

I work for an independent radio station called Radio Bremen.
Bremen is an old port near the mouth of the River Weser.
There are eight radio stations like ours in West Germany and
we are the smallest with 300,000 listeners.
WDR in Cologne has 5 million listeners.
I broadcast for 70 hours a month, playing records and
talking to people in the studio.
People aren't allowed to phone in or send requests
as they do in some other places.

Until recently most of our music came from Britain
and the USA and the groups sang in English, not German.
In the 1970s groups like Kraftwerk started a German
style of music but their words were still in English.
Now we have German music and German words.

I have a large collection of
rock, jazz and folk music.
I spend hours listening to
records and choosing those
I will play on my show

We have a mobile studio
which goes to about 40
live pop concerts a year.
These broadcasts are
very popular in Bremen.

Facts

Capital City   The capital city of West Germany
is Bonn.

Language   Most people in West Germany speak German
but there are regional dialects in
many parts, especially in the north.

Money   German people pay for things with
Deutsche Marks (DM) and Pfennigs.
There are 100 Pfennigs in 1 DM.

Churches   About half the people are Protestants
and half are Roman Catholics.

People   In 1982 there were 61,600,000 people
living in West Germany.

Weather   In the north and west the weather
is mild and damp.
In the south and east the winters
are cold and the summers fairly hot.

Government   West Germany is a federal republic
split into 10 regions, called *Länder*,
plus West Berlin.
The parliament in Bonn has 2 chambers,
the *Bundestag* and the *Bundesrat*
(see page 27).

Houses   One third of the people own houses and
                two thirds rent houses or flats.

Schools   Children spend four years at primary school.
                Then they go to a main school for
                5 or 6 years, to an intermediate school
                for 6 years, or to a *gymnasium* for 9 years
                (see page 17).

Farming   Most farms are quite small.
                Wheat, sugar beet, and potatoes are
                the main crops and many farmers
                rear cattle too.
                Forestry is also important.

Factories   Engineering is the most important industry.
                West German factories also produce
                steel, cars, ships, electrical goods,
                chemicals, and scientific equipment.
                Most of the factories are in the
                Ruhr Valley (see page 41).

News   There are 1,240 newspapers in West Germany
                and 600 of them are daily papers.
                There are three TV channels and
                two main radio stations, as well as
                local radio stations (see page 56).

Index